Your Full Potential: How to Overcome Fear and Solve Any Problem

Dan Desmarques

Published by 22 Lions Bookstore, 2020.

Table of Contents

Copyright Page 1

About the Publisher 3

Introduction 5

Chapter 1: How Do We Manifest Our Destiny? 7

Chapter 2: How Do We Overcome Negative Cycles? 11

Chapter 3: How Do We Win in Life Through God? 15

Chapter 4: How Do We Discover Our Full Potential? 19

Chapter 5: What is the Purpose of Our Encounters? 23

Chapter 6: Why Do We Procrastinate? 25

Chapter 7: How to Control Our Emotions? 27

Chapter 8: How to Overcome Frustration? 31

Chapter 9: How to Be More Positive? 35

Chapter 10: How to Defeat Your Enemies? 37

Chapter 11: How to Develop Discernment? 41

Chapter 12: How to Control Your Subconscious Mind? 45

Chapter 13: Why You Shouldn't Justify Yourself? 47

Chapter 14: How to Overcome Resentment? 51

Chapter 15: How to Confront Your Fears? 55

Chapter 16: How to End Negative Karma? 59

Chapter 17: How to Overcome Insults? 61

Chapter 18: Why is Love Overrated? 63

Chapter 19: How to Use Trauma to Your Advantage?..................................65

Chapter 20: How to Simplify Your Plans?...67

Chapter 21: Why Some People Will Always Fail?..69

Chapter 22: Why Do We Attract What We Don't Want?..............................73

Chapter 23: Why You Shouldn't Feel Ashamed?..75

Chapter 24: How to Challenge the Odds?..79

Chapter 25: Why Do People Lie to Themselves?...81

Chapter 26: How to Be Rich and Spiritual?...85

Chapter 27: How to Think Effectively?..87

Chapther 28: How to Solve Any Problem?...89

Chapther 29: How Can Negativity Be Good for You?..................................91

Chapter 30: How to Identify Your True Nature?..95

Copyright Page

Your Full Potential: How to Overcome Fear and Solve Any Problem

By Dan Desmarques

Copyright © Dan Desmarques, 2019 (1st Ed.). All Rights Reserved.

Published by 22 Publishing

About the Publisher

About the 22 Lions Bookstore:

www.22Lions.com

Facebook.com/22Lions

Twitter.com/22lionsbookshop

Instagram.com/22lionsbookshop

Pinterest.com/22lionsbookshop

Introduction

Many of us go through life without really knowing how much we can achieve. A big portion of our time is dedicated to solving problems and struggling against our own limitations.

We live far from our full potential. But why is it that some people achieve whatever they want and easily, while others don't?

I was asked this question many times, mainly in relation to myself, because most people couldn't understand how I was able to do so much in life and with good results all the time.

You see, the ones who succeed in achieving their goals, know which paradigms and values to follow. Most of these rules have been outlined in many books too, and throughout history, either for religious purposes, or to educate warlords and philosophers, and they can be resumed in simple principles, which we can see around us every day.

In this book, you will learn about such laws and rules and see how they challenge us and stop us from developing ourselves when not known. You will also learn precise mind techniques and hacks to use them effectively, so that you can achieve what you want much faster.

The proper application of this information will make it seem as if you have developed special powers and abilities that others don't consider possible. You will be able to look smarter and make faster decisions at work and in your personal life. You will also gain an upper level of perception in business and finance, and much more.

This information is based on old secrets, and is outlined here in a simple form, transversal to any area of life.

Chapter 1: How Do We Manifest Our Destiny?

The connection we all have to the cosmic energy, from which love is only a representation among many, allows detecting the projections of the ether in our being, among which we find our dreams.

This is why prayer, as in asking questions to a higher entity, is so important.

When we do that, we are connecting ourselves to that field, and in doing so, attracting more answers in the form of dreams, insights and ideas.

What is also interesting about this habit, shows itself in the old mystical arts, such as numerology. For people do tend to desire that which they were predestined to manifest.

In every single case in which I applied the concepts of numerology, I saw the same occurring: the people to whom I applied the knowledge were chasing happiness by following a path that had already been predisposed to them at birth.

I was doing the same. I was born to be a writer. But I was, nonetheless, avoiding it, because I didn't believe I should become one.

Took me only five years to write over three hundred books and make this come true. But took me more than fifteen years to accept that I should be a writer, considering the moment in which I realized it for the first time.

Even though there is free will, humans do tend to make decisions that fit their spiritual nature, reason why cartomancy and other esoteric sciences can be called effective studies of futurology when properly applied.

The paradigm of existence has no place for egotism, selfishness or punishment, because our spiritual path is always full of experiences that push us in the right way — by either moving us forward or making us realize something about our true self.

The occult sciences have been wrongly labeled as diabolical by many ignorant minds, but I am not saying either that they cannot be used to channel evil. Just as love can pull a narcissist into our life, or scare him or her away, the occult can also be used for good or evil too.

You see, God created both angels and demons, which means they come from the same source, and are gifted with the same type of wisdom. This wisdom is revealed in the natural order of things, which comes from the main source.

This is the type of knowledge that has been kept as a secret for thousand of years, precisely because it can be used for evil.

Sadly, the masses are more predisposed for evil now, due to the force of their ego, than they are for doing good, reason why anything can be used to reinforce such instincts.

The information and the tools, however, are neutral.

This said, even though cartomancy, as many other mystical arts, can be used for evil, as I have witnessed many times, the real purpose is introspection and the realization of the type of changes we must accept, in order to attract a more harmonious life, aligned with the Devine will.

Along this line of thought, it is only natural to observe that the greatest changes emerge from within when we align ourselves with the cosmic will.

Destiny can be more important than our capacity to change it, but with every decision, fate is altered, although not deviating from its original purpose — our consciousness.

The battle between free will and predestination is not related to the physical world, but only our internal world.

If, for example, we reject the one we were supposed to love, we'll learn what we would have to learn from this person with someone else.

YOUR FULL POTENTIAL

If the attraction was strong, we will suffer for a long time until we find someone else or something in life that fits our need to obtain the lessons we couldn't gain otherwise.

Sometimes, this occurs in a short period of time, and repeatedly, making us feel that we are riding a bad wave of negative karma. But, what it really means, is that we must understand something important and rapidly.

One of the most interesting things about bad karma, is that the righteous, who haven't abandoned the path of love while suffering, are always embraced by fate, through unexpected events that place them exactly where they should be.

The opposite occurs with those who thought that, by manipulating certain events and outcomes, would be in some type of advantage over others.

This drama is clearly played between narcissists and empaths. The narcissists are always caught by their karma, no matter what they do, or how smart they think they are. Their plans never really work as they thought they would. And that is one of the reasons behind their lethargy and lack of motivation in life. They feel that life never works according to their will. And yet, they can't look at themselves and see why, in order to change such results.

The less capable one is of introspecting himself on his actions, the more likely he is to become a victim of destiny.

Chapter 2: How Do We Overcome Negative Cycles?

Those who can't learn from the past, tend to find themselves repeating behaviors that determine a future that seems cyclical.

This happens because we seek experiences to bridge us to lessons that can somehow help us overcome our memories. It is in our nature to constantly bridge past and future.

We can't really change until we understand crucial things for our own development. That's why people who jump from relationship to relationship, seeking something outside of them, and that they themselves can't provide, typically find themselves in cycles of abandonment and betrayal.

One must then be able to look beyond what seems to occur, i.e., the words spoken and the aggression taking place, to seek within the cycle of repetition what has yet not been understood.

The most common lessons that people run from are attributed to self-love and self-respect. But these terms can't be properly assimilated if analyzed with the ego.

Self-love is what we show when choosing a companion and friends who reflect our potential, while addressing the behaviors that we must change in order to become better persons.

Self-respect is what you reflect, when rejecting someone who doesn't seem interested in promoting your best attributes and much less noticing them.

It is truly a waste of time to invest on someone who is not by our side when we are sick, and is not doing his or her best to improve the quality of our life; someone who doesn't truly see our well-being in an empathic manner and has no confidence in our capacities.

It is, nonetheless, difficult to find such personalities, because the large majority of the population is mentally and emotionally broken. They need affection and acceptance more than anything else. They are, to a great extent, emotionally immature too. That is why so many relationships are doomed to fail from the start.

In general, we deeply desire someone to free our spirit, we dream with love and love the ones we least expect, because love is a divine project that finds subconscious meanings, beyond our own visualizations. We hardly find anyone that escapes this willingness.

In a way, you can say that God will not allow you to meet someone that makes you happy without a challenge, but what kind of challenge should it be, if not connected to our own needs?

The spiritual challenges are usually related to aspects of our personality that must be surpassed. And so, the other person will address exactly those and very often reflect them too.

This is why the most spiritual ones tend to attract the most devastating of all emotional pains, in the form of individuals who are either not very empathetic or have a short life to live, or both.

Long-lasting happiness obtained from love is indeed possible, but only when the differences are accepted and both work towards facing the outside challenges instead of competing against one another.

By default, whenever we focus on what others think, we are more likely to fail.

The changes in our reality are composed mainly of three elements, and in a relationship, the third one tends to be external. Therefore, to focus on the thoughts of others, is to disregard our own goals, allowing them to weaken over time.

Any quarrel between lovers is nothing but a deception on the long process of transmutations that where allowed by connecting to those who had negative intentions.

YOUR FULL POTENTIAL

When a relationship is strong enough to develop on its own, nothing and nobody can really stop it from growing in a healthy way.

That is why we can also attribute the high numbers on divorce rates to lack of willingness in a mutual cooperation and acceptance between the individuals in the relationship.

It is, foremost, the refusal to operate as a team, that leads to frustration and divorce.

On the other hand, as mentioned above, it is inevitable that focusing on the needs of others, outside of our own personal life, will always tend to attract inner conflicts related to our own identity and values.

Chapter 3: How Do We Win in Life Through God?

The surrendering before the sacred designs of the divine doesn't imply a total submission to impulses, but a constant awareness towards the reasons behind them.

Existence requires a permanent balance between what is done and the knowledge about why. At least, so that any action can make sense and decisions become more effective over time.

Only fools would say that freedom implies a complete unconsciousness, for never someone who is unaware of his own actions will truly be free.

The most obvious example comes from the abuse of drugs, alcohol and other substances, as they represent a deliberate separation of consciousness. On the other hand, the less active a being is towards his own spiritual path, the more he will feel the need to express himself sexually, which will turn into another form of addiction.

Those who are detached from their spirit, tend to attract not only one problem or addiction, but many, as if going downhill in life.

Even the energy of the body is never stable, but relative to how we channel it.

Along this line, love or lust, quite often appears as the guiding force among the masses.

There is actually a correlation between fear, lust, and self-abasement. Because, the more someone is unconscious, or quite simply, disconnected from his higher self — his potential in life —, the more likely this person is to allow his impulses to guide him, and the more he will suffer whenever this is not fulfilled.

It is for this reason that narcissists tend to suffer so much with their own ego. They cannot fulfill themselves beyond the most elementary need of admiration and acceptance through lust.

Nonetheless, it is also normal that, in a world lacking a higher spiritual awareness and love, sex takes on a bigger role, in order to force consciousness through lust and frustration.

Now, this may not make much sense to most people, but understand that, after lust comes attachment, and after attachment comes commitment, or the need to be loved and accepted.

Although it is not normal in any way that two strangers decide to have sex — and even though this has been normalized by the current values of our society —, it is normal that they may find themselves attached after that, and seeking to create a connection that should exist prior to sex itself.

The question we can then ask is: can we create love out of lust?

Probably, we can, otherwise lust would not exist. But that's like seeking spirituality through its opposite. It is as if we had acquired the ability to reason and think for no purpose. Because, after all, sex with strangers is what animals do.

That inner void that appears when we lack love, can't be fulfilled only with sex. There must be an empathic connection unfolding, as well as the vanishing of anxiety towards trust for that to happen.

As spiritual beings, we can't deny our perpetual evolution and needs beyond our physical body. That attitude always brings devastating consequences.

The changes that occur in our moral values as a society then, don't really change the eternal laws of happiness and love. But we must adjust to them in order to fulfill our own goals. And for that, we need to develop a higher capacity for forgiveness.

I can't say that this is easy to do. It is very difficult. I have met many beautiful women willing to develop a stable relationship with me, but I could not forgive their past of whoring over multiple men. They made me feel as if I was about to marry a prostitute.

YOUR FULL POTENTIAL

You see, many times our values clash against each other, forcing us to prioritize one over the other, or simply, readjust them. And that, in the world we have today, is becoming extremely difficult.

For example, the more women aggressively defend their right to sleep with whomever they want, the wider the number of men who will want nothing to do with them.

You can't fight biology with reason. And quite often, biology has better reasons than our own. Because, you see, many scientific studies are not being done or allowed to prove something that the masses refuse to know, but if such was the case, and science wasn't always paired with social will, we would come to the conclusion that there is a correlation between mental disorders, lack of empathy, and the amount of sexual partners one has, especially for the female gender.

Marriage is, many times, seen a form of validating an irresponsible behavior, because it doesn't make any sense when it removes all rights from one gender to provide them to another. That is, at the very least, extortion and emotionally abuse.

You see, many people battle religious dogma and morals, as a way to affirm and reinforce their identity, but plenty of what has been segregated into the religious groups, is rooted in universal laws that safeguard our mental health, as well as our financial health.

Chapter 4: How Do We Discover Our Full Potential?

All that is part of our reality, from objects to people, is composed of energy. But thought, is also in itself also composed of energy.

When we create a thought, we release a vibration of energy which will interconnect with other surrounding forms of energy. Thus, we can then say that the limits of the physical reality only exist in our perception of it.

The more you know, in the spiritual sense — as in spiritual acknowledgement, the less dependent of the physical reality and its outcomes, you become.

The more interconnected the world seems to you, the less you will depend on it.

As a matter of fact, one of the greatest achievements of my life, was not in gaining the freedom to be whomever I choose to be, or go where I want, and do what I feel, but to realize that, a greater detachment from the physical world, brings forth a greater sense of interconnection that few can understand at the same time.

In other words, I became much more than I thought I could be, while also having more difficulties in being understood by others. And I now care more about other people than they often do about themselves.

My ways of expressing love and empathy are often ruled out as tyrannical and judgmental, because that's how people react to help that contradicts their beliefs.

On the other hand, it is very difficult for me to explain myself to others.

It's hard for me to answer questions such as "where are you from" and "what do you do for for a living", because I change so fast, and can do so many things, that it's impossible, even for myself, to be able to describe such potential in a limiting way.

Another example of this state of mind appears when someone asks me: "How long will you stay in this city?"; or "Why did you come here?". Because, I am so connected to the future, that I can't possible label my actions based on the present.

I can't state clearly the reasons why I am in a certain city until I know them. I can only answer why I left the previous city where I was before.

If I could actually answer this question, I would be closing myself for the possibilities ahead of me.

Few know that is very easy to explain whatsoever we did in the past to reach a certain result — good or bad. But the truth is that, when we were there, in that moment, we didn't really know what type of outcome we would get.

The last time this occurred, was when I was living in Warsaw — Poland. Just weeks later, after arriving, I started a relationship with someone I never predicted to meet. And several weeks after that, it was over; I received two amazing offers from Krakow and a small town in Croatia, in front of the ocean, plus a bunch of new business offers from old friends in Asia. Meaning that, if I had limited myself, I wouldn't be prepared for all that, especially, the losses and disappointments.

The reason why so many of us suffer with our failures, is because we are closed to our potentialities.

In my case, I had left Lithuania before moving to Poland, because I was feeling sad after a relationship came to an end. And I started a new one soon after, just by moving to a new country. And I really liked both girls, but the last one was not ready to commit to a person like me.

However, I then found greater opportunities to increase the meaning of my life and reach my purposes even faster than before, and simply by being true to myself.

You see, the more you connect yourself to this infinite source of blessings — the sacred geometry of life —, the more you realize that you never really lose anything. You are simply moving forward. And, if the ones you encounter are in

YOUR FULL POTENTIAL

the same boat, willing to share those potentialities with you, they will definitely be part of your journey; otherwise, you have to leave them behind, in their own little world.

Chapter 5: What is the Purpose of Our Encounters?

Few people know why they found us, and no amount of explanation can help them see that which they don't want to see.

Another of the greatest lessons in my life, came from reencountering former girlfriends many months after we were apart. I realized that, in every single situation, they had regretted their decision. And why? Because they made decisions based on fears, rooted in their needs, rather than my potential or the potential of the relationship.

They did not believe in a future with me. And then saw me getting better, every single time, when it was already too late and I wouldn't take them back.

I couldn't. They were attached to a person that did not exist anymore. And they moved on by starting other relationships that they considered more advantageous for them.

That made me realize something else about myself: I change much faster than anyone else, by simply neglecting my fears, and focusing on the potential future ahead of me.

It's this focus on a dream, a goal, a prospect, that changes me, despite any outcome.

Faith is a great source of strength that many lack. And when you are abandoned by those you trusted, this faith gains a deeper meaning, because it's all you have to keep moving forward.

The foolish thing for me to do, would be to try to keep that which holds me back, namely, women who complain about a life I must commit to in order to achieve my goals.

Remember this: God does not make you or anyone suffer; He simply removes from your life that which is holding you back from achieving what you want.

If you regret your losses, it is only because you have focused on the wrong things. And God will want you to know that too, by cornering you against your true self, until you learn this lesson.

A person who regrets her past, has certainly made the wrong decisions. But looking at those decisions won't change anything. It's the values behind the decisions that truly determine the potential that a person has to change.

You see, if a woman leave a man because he was poor, and he then becomes rich, she was looking at the wrong things. If she leave him because she didn't believe in his potential to grow, she was being impatient. And, if she listens to people who do not have her best interests in sight, despite the fact that her partner is doing his best to make her happy, again, she has followed the wrong values.

For most people, these values are subdivided in two groups - religious and non-religious. But such idea is just part on another illusion.

Many people have asked me to describe God, in order to understand how I think. But it's not possible to resume in a few words what or whom God is. God is a codeword for a multi-versed perspective. For some it means Good, Optimism and Deliverance; for others is Greatness, Open-mindedness and Dedication; for many others is Geometry, Operation and Data; and for some is Greed, Obsession and Death. But all perspectives lead to the same outcome and you don't need to meet an architect to live in the house he created.

Everyone is following a G.O.D. of their own. We only need to see if that God is our own.

Once you learn your lessons, you will then shift your perspective of G.O.D., and come closer to Him — the real God, while reinforcing your faith. And in doing so, you will be reaching your dreams faster than anyone else.

Every single billionaire in the world shares the same habits, most of which include this G.O.D. in them: they reinforce their faith, every single day, with visualizations. Their path is the same as the path of anyone else. They simply move faster in the acknowledgement that we all change in the same direction.

Chapter 6: Why Do We Procrastinate?

The greatest potential that a human being can reach is related to the conception and transformation of a reality merely with the exercise of thought. But how can he do that unless he understands the sacred parameters of such reality? And how can he study them without studying himself and his environment?

What can be known is always part of the psychic environment — personal universe — and the interpretation is always subjective.

This mystical paradigm assumes deeper connections with those who have a greater importance on a personal and emotional level in our life.

A person is then composed of this network of influences that merge in many spectrums of his being.

To a certain extent, we are as much as those who know us may allow us to be and accept on their own individual context. And many of our thoughts are actually theirs.

We think what others think about us. We cannot be separated by this constant fact manifesting within our mind. Our vibrational energy is interconnected with the vibrational energy of others.

Now, this puts everything to a whole new level of responsibility and realism, because you don't want to be associated with those who are wasting their life and focusing their thoughts on entertainment rather than setting goals.

The ability to control our own thoughts is then also the ability to control the flow of thoughts in others towards us and how it affects us.

It is for this reason that we can say the following: if you wish to control others and master them, learn first to control and master yourself. If you are king of your own mind, you will be independent of the outside world as well.

If you cannot control your own mind, anyone can control you, directly or indirectly.

As a matter of fact, I have met many intelligent people who cannot control their own mind. They believe that being smart consists in having many thoughts. And so, they allow themselves to be polluted with the thoughts of others. And in doing so, they corrupt their own thoughts, and make very stupid decisions.

It's interesting to observe that without this knowledge, even the smartest ones can do the most imbecile things.

On the other hand, I also noticed that such individuals are as reckless in choosing their friends, as they are in controlling their own thoughts.

The outer and the inner reality arise through both conscious and subconscious agreements. They are interconnected. We change by either compromising or accepting whatsoever is give to us. We also can't truly create anything that hasn't first been imagined by someone and predicted by a majority. And so, what makes us who we are, is the direction in which we channel our will or the lack of it.

Once you realize this, it should be obvious that the most creative minds assume a pioneering and extremely important role for the future of mankind, as from the moment they show the world a new opportunity, it begins to be accepted immediately, even if subconsciously predicted at first. They change the realm in which we interact by dreaming new worlds and making them factual.

Many world records that were first thought to be impossible to break, started being broken once one person did it. Because, suddenly, it became a possibility for others. And although many have thought that flying would be an impossibility, and many still don't know how airplanes really fly with so much weight, that doesn't stop millions of people from flying between countries.

Artists, scientists and entrepreneurs don't have the credit and respect they deserve, because with much difficulty, they carry the entire planet on their back throughout their entire existence.

Chapter 7: How to Control Our Emotions?

We can notice that the ones who oppose our dreams, will manifest a type of energy that will block us from manifesting them. And even we can do this with ourselves, when allowing ourselves to believe what others think of us, or when focusing on those external judgements.

A thought will more quickly be welcomed by those who are emotionally close to it; and so, quite a lot of what people decide about themselves and their future, comes from their closest friends and relatives.

In fact, "Man is the only a creature whose emotions are entangled with his memory" (Marjorie Holmes). And this means that we have been evolving as a collective, a group of communities based on agreements.

When we think, we are passing on knowledge that can be received by anyone else, because the energy grid in which the thoughts interconnect is shared by all human beings on the planet. No thought is independent or hidden from the collective subconscious. But only self-aware individuals can access this network with relative ease; and it takes practice before you can clearly see which thoughts are yours, which are not, and which ones are inspired by the Devine, or God.

Creative individuals can exercise this ability at the highest levels and imagination is the most practical tool to develop such competence. The more you can imagine yourself in a new life, one you wish for yourself, the more developed you will be in the art of building your personality according to your dreams and then shifting reality in that same direction.

There is a constant exchange of energy that vibrates around the planet and affects us emotionally and psychologically. And this exchange can be measured in frequency and strength.

The stronger the emotions, the more impact the energy field will have in the effects created. A strong emotion generates more magnetic force, ether it comes from those who love us or the ones who hate us the most.

Therefore, it is our focus and our guided will, that assures that our goals are achieved despite anyone opposing them.

Once your will is strong enough, you will actually notice more people in your environment trying to stop you. And this happens, because your confidence has become threatening to them.

I have had people telling me that they hate me and they don't know why.

The why is easy for me to explain, but not for them to understand: I vibrate at a much higher frequency. Because my level of creativity and spirituality is very high.

Whenever someone comes in contact with me, this person is changed by the force of my field. And if this same person is in contact with many people who are pushing in the opposite direction, she will naturally resent me instead, even though the normal thing to do would be to reject all of her friends.

People always choose the side of the majority. Because their tribalistic brain tells them that survival is in that behavior. And that's how they make the most stupid decisions based on instinct and then justify them, in order to avoid looking at themselves as common idiots.

If you want to learn how to control your emotions, you must first be aware of your instincts. They don't always operate in your favor. Instincts are always working by default.

- At a first level, you have primitive instincts guiding your reason;

- Then, you have your emotions, reinforcing such instincts, after your reasoning led you to certain direct experiences, most of which, caused by you;

- Finally, you have a justification of the outcome, blindfolding you to your true self, so that you never realize that you made decisions based on fear rather than logic.

YOUR FULL POTENTIAL

The more unconscious people are of this cycle, the more likely they are to apply what in psychology is labeled as a projection: When people judge others based on who they really are.

Chapter 8: How to Overcome Frustration?

Sometimes, and despite the best intentions, people get lost in the pain of others and end up suffering with their own negative emotions and thoughts of self-doubt. That is why the consciousness of good and evil — as well as the perception of evil in what seems good — and the way both energies interact, is so important in order to cultivate a healthy mindset. Our happiness depends on it.

It is very difficult to create positive outcomes out of positive actions when our emotions seem to go against this flow of energy.

If you are working very hard on a project but fighting with your spouse, for example, you will likely see your projects fail in many ways that you never imagined possible.

In almost every toxic relationship I had, I only saw my income increasing dramatically once they ended, and despite the pain that such ending caused on both parties.

The entire transformation from negative to positive in our results, implies a relearning composed of challenges, which force us to clear the mind of false beliefs, in a process that induces psychological suffering, as nobody likes to feel lost and disturbed by confusion. But there is no greater loneliness than the one we feel when realizing we have been wrong in our path and for too long.

We work very hard to escape confronting past mistakes, and in doing this, we sabotage our future.

Happiness depends on a subjective perspective that keeps changing within its own cycles. We change our path as much as we change ourselves. We never know what truly makes us happy until we experience the outcome of what we thought would lead us towards that emotional state. And we often cry over things we did not really want.

Our brain has a way of deceiving our memories, because we are emotional creatures. Our survival depends as much on our finances as it does on our emotions.

We instinctively know that we can't be motivated while feeling miserable. That's why our brain changes our memories, to make them match our current willingness.

It may seem like magic what I am about to tell you, but truly amazing and liberating if you apply it: If you focus, every single day, on the future you want, you will not be depressed, you won't have thoughts unrelated to what you want, and, if you are dealing with a breakup or some form of disappointment, it will all vanish, simply because your mind can't process two contradictory emotions at the same time, i.e., the one you are producing towards an hypothetical future, and the one you produce related to the fear of not getting it.

Psychologists could help much more people by helping them talk about the future instead of the past.

Most of them are not even qualified as human beings to judge anyone's past. They know little more about life than common sense, and often not even that, reason why their results are so poor.

The reason why many millionaires and billionaires love their work is as important as why love keeps them rich. If that wasn't the case, they would demotivate once achieving their financial goals and simply waste their fortune in futilities.

As a matter of fact, I would say that one of the most obvious differences between the rich and the poor, is that the poor work for money. They don't really like to work. They enslave themselves in order to survive, to pay for their rent and their food, and especially to have more comfort in their life, in the form of more possessions.

It requires a very different mindset, to work for something greater than ourselves, to work for pleasure rather than money, and to commit and sacrifice to a goal that isn't immediately present, and may even lead us to bankruptcy and homelessness. That is why entrepreneurs, just as artists, are always taking the biggest risks. And yet, instead of admiration, the masses often despise them and label them as crazy.

Our world is not perfect, but the imperfection is a perfect match to the mindset of the masses. You can't change the world because you can't change billions of people, and force them to do something they don't want. That is tyranny. And the reason why tyranny has such a bad reputation, is because people never saw good tyranny. Good tyranny, would be to murder the stupid, evil and lazy, and award the compassionate, empathetic and kind.

Unless you have seen someone awarding the kind and punishing the evil, you have not seen a good person. The large majority is guided by fear, and then rationalizes this fear to quiet their ego.

Chapter 9: How to Be More Positive?

In order to experience what is positive in a greater proportion, we need to search within ourselves and know how to identify the positive path of life from a subjective standpoint.

That is like trying to find your way out of a forest in the dark, without any device to help you. The fear of being killed by a wild animal is equivalent here to the fear most of us have of losing our wealth or becoming sick and incapable of working.

So, how do we find our way out of this situation?

You can look at this analogy from a personal viewpoint, as many situations repeat themselves, even between reincarnations, to teach us specific lessons.

The three and main things you can use to help yourself are: faith, focus and persistence. You can't stop, you can't doubt, and you certainly can't lay down and rest.

Most likely, the most idiotic thing I hear all the time, and in different cultures, from the vast majority, as an answer to any type of life problem is: slow down and take a rest.

History is full of stupid decisions made by the masses, and the consequences are quite obvious.

Surrendering your emotions to randomness and luck is certainly one of them.

The brightest among us don't always seem so as well. One of the most common mistakes that the thirstiest for knowledge tend to do, consists in ignoring what is positive in order to experience more. They then focus on the accumulation of errors and mistakes, but are rarely fulfilled.

In the previous example, it would be the equivalent to spending more nights in the forest to learn to overcome fear, rather than simply leaving the forest.

Many of such brave and smart, but very stupid souls, have perished into oblivion and contributed little to our current lifestyle. Just consider how many Europeans died in wars to protect borders that are now opened to prioritize financial and business transactions.

One way or another, the world is always forced towards where it should go. The "why" is only in our mind.

In a way, it may seem that many have encountered fulfillment in their own acknowledgement of a subjective truth, and yet they pay for the outcome with a tremendous emotional imbalance, often leading to negative states, such as loneliness, alienation and depression.

The one who is eager to know the world may never feel at home anywhere. He is seeking outside what he can't recognize within himself. That is the cause for the imbalance.

The stages of development beyond the majority of the world are extremely challenging.

Chapter 10: How to Defeat Your Enemies?

The desire to know more is not in itself negative, but, like a forbidden fruit in a paradise, when we drive the spirit to pleasure with the aim of just living that emotion, we lose control of its innate purity — the purpose we were born with.

It is for this reason that we require discipline in our path, in order to channel our best interests — our true nature.

In fact, more and more people, claim that it was the discipline they found, either in martial arts, the military or any other similar activity, that brought them closer to their goals.

Pleasure is intrinsic to the spirit but always comes with a desire for self-expression, reason why all will must be channeled through technique, focus and determination — skills that must be mastered.

In other words, the knowledge that enriches the spirit towards self-development is the same leading to happiness and true fulfillment, but can only be found through a spiritual alignment.

The alternative tends to lead to egotism and a self-deceptive sense of pride. And this, may then lead to a view of society as being a threat to the survival of the self-portrayed image — the ego.

The cycle then necessarily continues with the identification of the evil and the need to fight it, even if it is self-created.

Many studies in psychology have found that we are predisposed to justify our own past by replicating it in the present. Habits do reinforce themselves over time.

Few people stop to think about the meaning behind their own beliefs.

When I was teaching martial arts, a common question students asked me was: "How do you defend yourself from multiple attackers?"

My answer was always very simple: "By not being where they are."

You see, whatever is the martial art chosen or the techniques learned, it is common knowledge among professional martial artists, that the most effective methods are always based on strategy. But what kind of strategy?

In the most aggressive sports, like boxing or mixed martial arts, it is known that a good defense is as important as a powerful attack, but more important is to know how to avoid the attacks of your opponent without having to defend them.

Naturally, from this point of view, many techniques and principles were developed, and different martial arts may vary in how they see it. But a common agreement maintains: you can't do much for yourself by simply being in front of your attacker.

The same applies to evil. You will never possess enough knowledge to defeat it. The knowledge you acquire only becomes useful when directed at a meaningful and enlightening purpose.

The sense of security that an evil person may possess is always delusional too. This person is already setting her fate in the wrong direction by not making the right decisions, namely, towards changing her entire life in order to become a better person.

In all the cases in which I found people who quit drugs and alcohol, and decided to become committed to improving themselves, I saw the same: they all had a higher goal to justify it, to channel their energy and knowledge. And that goal was always the love of others or simply the love of their own family.

Sadly, many people do choose the wrong side of life, when not feeling that type of love at home. But they can change themselves later in life, when recognizing such love in the family that they created for themselves with their spouse.

Any form of narcissism can be healed with the acceptance of love. The question is: can a narcissist accept love? Because if he can, he won't be a narcissist any longer.

YOUR FULL POTENTIAL

The reason why narcissists are narcissists and psychopaths are psychopaths, and people go through life suffering from the same problems for many years, is because they have not looked at the thought patterns keeping them there, in the "punching zone".

Chapter 11: How to Develop Discernment?

One of the greatest attributes acquired through a consistent moral action is discernment. Those who follow righteousness, do become more sensitive to the variances in the energy field around them.

That is something that a person who has spent too much time in fabricating thoughts rooted on the ego can hardly do. The evil ones are too proud to admit that they can't even recognize a good person when seeing one.

Quite often, they don't believe such people exist. And so, they persist in their beliefs, while setting themselves apart from happiness furthermore. Because, you see, the ones who don't believe in happiness, can't believe in the opportunities that lead them there, and typically push such opportunities away as well.

It is paradoxically interesting, that narcissists, for example, are as attracted to other narcissists as they are attracted to empaths, because of what both represent — vanity in one case and virtue in the other, i.e., the fear and the need at the same time.

It may seem tragic to realize that narcissists are made, but not as tragic as realizing that the reason why they can't heal, is because they can't be happy or accept the happiness of others. They make their partners miserable, and in doing so, attract misery towards themselves. And this, because they have normalized their own misery, and their own behavior patterns are a result of such normalization.

They lack the capacity to discern long-term value and short-term pleasure.

As a matter of fact, it is the inadequacy towards change that keeps them mentally sick. They are stuck inside the traumas of their childhood.

Many of us, one way or another, also allow ourselves to be stuck inside our own bubble of traumas. And that karmic ball of energy keeps stealing our discernment away, in the form of positive amounts of energy that is wasted in the avoidance of a past that has already happened.

Most of us are too afraid of a repetition of the past to consider a potential future. And yet, that negativity isn't outside our control, but within it. We can take its power away by focusing on building a new life.

Those who are too afraid of what others think and worried about their own appearance, however, have surrendered to that mechanism operating in their subconscious mind, called "fear of the past".

They are not as afraid of others as they are afraid of their own inadequacy.

It is important to know, however, that spiritual sickness does lead to darkness — the refusal of the truth, the fear of consciousness, and the fear to love and be loved. That fear of the light occurs because, as with any other form of light, it reveals the ruins within a person.

It always amazed me to realize, for example, that those who are wicked, wish to see that wickedness in others. They seem to be attracted to people who are somehow broken, and places that are abandoned. It is as if they were seeking themselves through their own experiences. But, in doing so, they are trying to learn to forgive themselves.

Meanwhile, they can't do that, because they can't accept their own evil self. They have distanced themselves from their real persona far too much and for too long. And eventually, they hold on to a huge amount of rage within themselves that they can't deal with and end up projecting on others - the scapegoats.

A very angry but irrational person, is almost always redirecting self-hatred.

In view of this, any good therapeutical method must follow three phases: The capacity to reach self-awareness; the willingness to do it; and the process of reconstructing the identity with the right data.

This may seem simple. However, as I have come to realize with many personal experiences, most of the people who live in the dark, have destroyed themselves too much and associated themselves with the wrong personalities for long enough, to still maintain the capacity to change.

YOUR FULL POTENTIAL

In their need to belong and have friends, and be seen as normal by society, they have suppressed everything in habits that somehow delude their suffering, i.e., alcohol and drugs abuse with friends, endless hours of watching television and sleeping, and a constant anxiety towards finding new sexual partners to gain validation.

It is not possible to help them, without separating them from that world, and naturally, such world will put a fight against anyone trying to "separate" the one who needs help.

That war then becomes a mental war for the person in question, who is forced to make a decision. And as we know, most of the times, they choose to self-destroy.

Even if they do accept to follow a procedure, they are then often faced with an extremely incompetent therapist that does further damage, as it is the case with nearly all the therapists I have ever encountered.

It is easy to quit, quite simply, because most of the help offered in the world is in itself another form of self-destruction, or abused by sick minds hiding themselves behind socially acceptable and respected titles.

There should actually be an international court set precisely to deal with abuses on the field of mental health, because they are too common to be ignored.

Chapter 12: How to Control Your Subconscious Mind?

The memories that can't be recalled at a conscious level are constantly being associated with ideas of present time, controlling the conscious actions of the individual. But does it really exist such thing as a conscious and subconscious mind?

In truth, a large portion of what we name as subconscious, is manifesting in our emotions, and these are very conscious to us. Therefore, one should be able to differentiate the emotions that are justifiable at a present moment from those that aren't.

We want to think that human beings are conscious enough to do that, but the vast majority isn't.

What the masses do by default, consists in justifying any emotion by actually changing the circumstances in favor of the personal perception, rather than using the experiences to actually heal.

That is why the narcissist must bully his spouse and children. He needs them to react in such a way that his anger against himself can be redirected towards them and justified, therefore also justifying his emotions, which will be the same ones that he wants to cause in others.

That is how a very egotistical person denies his or her own insanity.

You can notice, to a certain extent, that every behavior that has no exact explanation is controlled at a subconscious level. The person is dramatizing something that she has experienced before, most likely as a victim.

This fact alone, allows us to clearly state that, the vast majority of the human race is asleep, and not really in a state of consciousness. That is why so many attach themselves to the routines and habits that deny any need for a significant change.

They then demand and expect the government to take care of them, because quite frankly, they are too scared to do that themselves.

It is by far much easier to protest against unemployment and low salaries than it is to start a business of your own or to become a freelancer, always seeking for new clients. But the world in which we live doesn't offer much more options, unless you are an artist and you have cultivated your skills for a long period of time.

I notice this situation in my personal life as well. Most people don't believe I can write so many books, because they can't accept the fact that I have been reading encyclopedias on psychology and spirituality since I am a teenager, practicing various techniques of meditation since I am twelve years of age, and participating in meetings of different religious groups since I am five years old.

That is far too much for their small egotistical brain, with a vast number of wasted years, to comprehend. And so, ignorant as they are, the vast majority hates, distrusts and criticizes, even if what they say makes no sense.

They don't know that it makes no sense, because they are not aware.

They don't know that what they see and think makes no sense because their lack of logic is part of their own little world too; a world composed of webs of idiotic thoughts that somehow find a match among the idiotic thoughts of those they spend time with.

Chapter 13: Why You Shouldn't Justify Yourself?

I have spent the last years of my life, more often than not, trying to prove that I am a writer, instead of talking about what I write.

In most parts of the world, this reality is too far from the level of consciousness of the majority. The stupider a population, the more difficult for them to conceive a perception that is distinct from theirs.

That is why it's not an exaggeration to say that the Portuguese, the Spanish, the Lithuanians, the Latvians, the Estonians and the Polish, are, to a great extent, very stupid.

You see, you can always adjust reality to make it seem pleasant, as when we use the words large to describe fat, or disadvantageous to describe retarded, or different to describe ugly, but you won't be of much of a help for yourself or others by doing that, and you won't change reality either in that way.

I used to call my students stupid and they always felt outraged. But I was also the only teacher that ever helped them become much smarter than they were, and achieve all their goals in life, including creating their own business.

I only wish I had a teacher, during my entire life, or even one friend, that actually gave me a business idea in one hour only of talking to me, a business idea that always and every single time, succeeded, even if it was a different one for everyone.

I didn't see much appreciation in any of them, because, again, most people are also too stupid to notice who helped them the most.

Quite often, the teacher that could sing in the classroom and lie about his past received much more recognition.

People are indeed too dumb for their own good.

Many students did say that I was the best teacher they ever met. But that's still an overstatement in regards to someone that literally removed them from one karmic cycle and placed them in another, much higher, with only a few words.

Among all of these stories, the correlation between one situation and another appears as consciousness.

As I always told them: 'Unless you admit that you are stupid, you won't put efforts towards becoming smarter. And that is why I am here: to not only judge you but make you much better, according to my own judgement. Because, if my judgment is correct, you will win in life, and you will accomplish anything you want.'

My judgement was correct. I may have caused the greatest headaches they ever had, but many kept saying I was best teacher they ever had many years later, after studying in many other countries, including the United States, Spain, France, England and Germany. They never again met a teacher like me, and they never will, for obvious reasons, that are irrelevant to outline here in their full extent.

The truth is, most people are lucky to be alive. Most people don't really possess the skills required to survive. And the risk of keeping them alive is too high for what they can give in return to society.

This is why the topic of the basic income has become so important nowadays among politicians from around the globe.

From a spiritual point of view, we do see here why so many reincarnate on earth and replicate the same traumas and dramas of previous lives. It's from this perspective that several theories emerged describing planet earth as a prison for the worst souls of the universe.

This prison is made of a complex and, yet, a flexible system, that allows leaving at any moment, depending on the potential one has to liberate himself from the attachments of guilt and resentment.

This is not an unfair system in which many are doomed.

YOUR FULL POTENTIAL

The unfairness of our condition has been created and maintained by humanity over itself.

At a personal level, you can only escape it by being more than what surrounds you. This is why books like the one you are reading right now are so important. This type of books cross the universe of energy in which you are immersed.

Chapter 14: How to Overcome Resentment?

Guilt and resentment are low states of consciousness and they can't be addressed directly because they feed from fear.

Let's consider, for example, the case of a woman who was hurt by her father as a child. She may resent this event and forever fear commitment with any man she encounters. Whenever a relationship demands more commitment, she feels this threat. And the threat must be justified in her mind.

As a result, not only will she choose a man that she can easily control, either sexually or intellectually, or both, but also punish men who seem happier than her, more successful or too independent, because those three attributes awaken her own fears.

Many of these women can't even accept sexual positions that imply submission towards a man.

They will, nonetheless, separate their emotions from the sexual desire, an attitude that commonly leads towards promiscuity.

Women who come from traumatic backgrounds in their childhood do tend to become more promiscuous.

On the other hand, they often want a man that expresses himself emotionally and clearly, because they consider this type of man to be easier to control, observe and study. Such man makes them feel safer.

They also, nonetheless, consider him weaker, precisely for being so transparent. And so, here we have the reason why artists and empaths attract narcissists all the time, and why narcissists are attracted to them but also simultaneously hate them.

The saddest thing about such personalities is that they do spend an entire lifetime in the dark, never truly being able to understand and feel love. And this, because they are prioritizing an irrational need for security, based on a fear that is no longer justifiable by any state of sanity.

Many of them accept their condition over time, and turn to alcohol, drugs and a higher anxiety towards sex, as a way to compensate for their loneliness, depression and sense of unworthiness. The problem with such escapes is that they also consist in suppressing furthermore the impact of what has already been suppressed before, increasing in such way the power of the subconscious mind and limiting awarenesses to a higher level.

That is why many therapists claim that narcissism has no cure. You can't cure that which you run away from.

The egotistical ones eventually succumb to their own mental illnesses for the rest of their life, when believing that they are stronger by denying their own emotions.

This attitude may provide them with a temporary relief, but also steals the potential for happiness away.

There is then an increased need for fulfillment in these individuals, often channeled through work and admiration, as a way to recharge the mind with an energy that is being stolen away by the subconscious mind, in the form of thoughts, anger and misdirected rage. But a person heavily controlled by the subconscious can hardly accomplish anything. And here we have, the dilemma of the narcissist taking place: they seek those whom they hate, due to jealousy and envy; and they seek energy supply that they eventually waste.

This is what a distorted sense of admiration causes when one hates that which he wants to love, or fears that which he himself creates, i.e., abandonment.

Everything that darkness is can be resumed to a hatred of what is greater, more compassionate and pure. And further along this line, you can resume it in the compulsive act of self-destroying oneself, by pushing away that which one needs the most.

When deprived from such vital energy, the narcissist begins a process of self-abasement, for his body of energy weakens. He will then develop psychological obsessions but also more organic illnesses.

YOUR FULL POTENTIAL

Even worse is to consider that this situation doesn't end in one lifetime, because it eventually becomes karmic.

Chapter 15: How to Confront Your Fears?

Generally speaking, the stronger the feelings, the less likely it is that we are able to identify the cause. Quite simply, because the emotions control our reasoning.

This is common when we are afraid or in love. The emotions we feel overwrite our perceptions and make it difficult to act in a reasonable way.

The less aware someone is of such occurrences, the most likely it is that this person will interact with other people, and even make important life decisions, based on the past rather than a desirable future. And it is for this reason that the vast majority of the masses lose important opportunities in their life. They are guided by emotions that rarely are correlated to what is happening in front of them.

Misfortune if often the result of emotions overwriting the thinking process, rather than necessarily lack of luck.

To believe that success is attributed to luck is actually naive.

That is why actions are so important when we want to change our fate. Actions are the process in which we consciously confront our own decisions. And it is for this reason too, that those who persist the most towards their goals, through labor and study, tend to reach them.

Because you see, it is only through action that you obtain a direct feedback that forces you to reflect on your own thoughts.

In psychology, this is known as metacognitive processing.

On the other hand, the older one gets, the harder it is to change the personality.

At one point, the entire structure of our personality is built on thought patterns, and these were mostly built on emotional memory patterns, largely composed of unanalyzed suffering and the avoidance of pain. These situations are comparable to building skyscrapers over swamps. Either we destroy the skyscrapers or the swamps will continue to consume parts of the buildings.

People in this state, live consistently preoccupied with death instead of life, because they're being consumed by their own memories and the effects of such memories.

We could say that the best cure for any disease is happiness, and its discovery lies in the activities that make us feel happy, but we won't find them if we don't have a personality to match our goals, and this personality can't be found within the lack of it.

To solve this problem, we must address the relationship between the conscious and the subconscious.

There's no such thing as a unconscious mind without a conscious mind, therefore all subconscious memories can be accessed at the conscious level.

The subconscious memories are there, in order to not be remembered, but can be accessed by the natural process of confronting them. And we do that by increasing our potential for confrontation, i.e., our courage level. And this is done through activities that bring us pleasure and success, even if in small doses.

It is always the successful personalities that can easily talk about their childhood and all of its challenges. You will hardly find someone who is losing in life doing that. He can't confront his failures without having to confront his current situation.

Ironically, on the other hand, those who accept their present moment problems also overcome them more quickly.

The habit of setting goals and achieving them, is one of the ways we do this, but we can only do that if we accept the need to do it, and the circumstances that lead us there. It can be running for a certain period of time, reading a certain amount of pages of a book every day, or, quite simply, deciding to say something kind and friendly to a certain amount of people on our way to work.

How hard can it be, to say, "You look good today", to a least three persons every day?

YOUR FULL POTENTIAL

You see, kindness does improve your own confidence and your own mood, and your sense of accomplishment, as well as your self-belief. When you are kind to others, you are exercising your capacity to control your own emotions, confront them, accept them and move beyond them, without letting them control you. And interestingly, when you make others happy, you also make yourself happier.

Chapter 16: How to End Negative Karma?

Whenever you respond to a negative experience, mentally, verbally, or simply, at an emotional level, you are connecting yourself with that experience. This is why it is so hard to let go of our negative cycles.

Very often, the only way to end a negative cycle is by focusing on a new one and investing our energy in it.

In other words, we don't fight, confront of avoid old cycles of negativity, but simply change our focus to new activities.

This can be done, for example, by joining a sports' group, to avoid thinking about a relationship we had before, listening to music to change our mood, listening to jokes to shift our mind from a bad day at work, and so on.

There are many ways to shift your mind from your problems and dissociate yourself from them. And the habit will eventually help you in changing your attention to things that matter the most.

As an author, I am extremely criticized. But I have found that most of the critics are rooted on envy. People hate to know that I can succeed as a full-time author. Basically, I am living a dream that they can't even imagine for themselves. And I know this, because I have accomplished many impossible things before, and saw the same type of behaviors every single time. But how do you go on with your day, when you are being hated?

By applying everything I mentioned before, but also by realizing that you are very likely to lose friends, and lots of them when doing that.

The emotions I awaken in others are so strong, that it's impossible not to lose friends all the time.

Fame is indeed a lonely place to be. The price you pay for being extraordinary at something is high. And so, the strategies I use to overcome loneliness, have to always be extraordinary as well.

For example, I have decided not to stay in any country for longer than six months at a time anymore. Because I make friends very fast, I start new relationships very fast, and at one point, instead of being supported, I am being hated, and stopped. In every single relationship I had, women tried to stop me from being a writer. It makes them feel insecure and vulnerable. My high level of independency and freedom, awakes the vulnerabilities and insecurities in them.

In a way, it is as if people admired the same things they avoid. And they want the things or people they wish to change.

Rarely, will someone change herself towards a new reality. People are more dedicated to making the outside world become convenient to their own laziness and lack of willingness to move from one situation into another.

Chapter 17: How to Overcome Insults?

The attacks others throw at high performance individuals, typically come first directed at the confidence.

I immediately know when a woman I just met is attracted to me, because she doesn't waste any time in trying to convince me to take a local job from nine to five. In others words, the more attracted she is to me, and the more confidence she sees in me, the more insecure she feels.

The only way for her to balance that, is by erasing my own freedom and lower my confidence. And well, this also comes many times in the form of insults. Women that fall in love with me, do insult me a lot, especially, when they can't get what they want.

Most people think that their enemies are those that oppose them and their plans, but very often, the enemy is closer to our heart — it's the person who wants to fulfill your own plans, the one who loves you and admires you, that attacks the most.

A great amount of insults directed at entrepreneurs and famous artists say more about those who insult that them.

Too many people want to destroy that which exposes their own weaknesses.

I realized this soon in my life, when I started becoming famous very fast. Thousands of people would text me messages of appreciation and admiration, but then, as soon as they met me in person, would try to obtain information that they could use to destroy my reputation.

This occurred with almost every single person I met, until I realized why famous people have to ignore the vast majority.

The vast majority is really, really, stupid, envious, and evil.

I have been famous in many areas of my life, and I thought that, as a writer, this situation would slightly change, but it didn't. My readers behave like anyone else, meaning that the less they know about me, the more they respect my work, and the more they know, the more they try to destroy my reputation. But why do people behave like this, instead of benefiting from the work being produced?

This happens, because, again, people want that which they deny.

It is like those who ask you for help, and then insult you when you help them.

The vast majority of the human race, is not yet at a level in which it can be helped. This help has to be indirect.

Fame is also overrated. You don't want to be famous in a world that is highly narcissistic and obsessed with money. But this is something that those who have never experienced fame in their life hardly understand.

You see, as soon as you start worrying about the type of photos you put on the internet, and what others think of them, you start losing yourself simultaneously.

I spend so many hours working on my books, music and business partnerships, that I simply don't have the time left to care about what others think. In fact, I let them judge themselves when they judge me. Because, when a person laughs at you, ridicules you, or insults you, that person is exposing herself instead. And you do want people to express their thoughts about you, rather than hiding them.

It is by living life that you end bad karma. Not by being afraid of it. Because karma is merely a word for cycles of responsibility over the outcomes of our decisions.

You don't really attract bad karma when you attract an insult. On the contrary, you are attracting an opportunity to get rid of an undesirable person that was secretly wanting you to fail.

Those who support your results and want to see you happy, will never criticize your lifestyle.

Chapter 18: Why is Love Overrated?

Love is overrated because you can't really be in a relationship with someone who is not working towards a common goal.

In the end, the cycles of short term relationships become too common, not because you want, but because you are pushed towards it, and forced to make decisions between chasing your dreams or succumbing to the fears of someone.

The same applies to the emotional rollercoasters in which we may find ourselves when trying to balance our work, emotions and social lifestyle.

All of this insanity on the side of society forces me to balance it by acting accordingly, and make myself look like I am the insane one. And obviously, many people assume that, if I am always traveling and always alone. They think I enjoy it.

Nobody will ever assume that I consider most people a complete garbage without any value as human beings.

Many were actually surprised when I publicly wrote that not replying my messages leads to being excluded from my life.

They never before took into account that ignoring someone texting them was a bad thing. They think it's normal, because they do it all the time.

We live in a world with such a low criteria on social interactions, that when you expect people to act like normal human beings, that seems too much.

A large portion of my decisions do come from having no other choice.

If I wish to continue being a full-time author, overcome the insults and paranoia, and attacks I get all the time, and always be high on life, happy, highly productive, and able to create new books with quality, or work on old books to edit them and improve them, I have to do the extraordinary, I have to move as much as possible, I have to interact with lots of people at the same time, I have to travel, see new places, challenge myself intellectually, and be extremely strong from a psychological point of view, to handle all the transitions, breakups and attempts at destroying my self-confidence.

I have to, basically, become super-human, super-smart, and super-fast at selecting those that I allow in my social circle.

The more motivated to exterior and superficial statements of worth a society is, the more this applies. Reason why I don't recommend anyone to develop a business in Europe, where the overall culture is extremely limited and dumbed-down.

As time goes by, you will also see the struggle getting harder to overcome. By the time you are in your 40s, you will probably become very cynical, if you have met many thousands of people.

On the other hand, there are moments in which I feel a deep despair and even horror and fear. But I can't stop anymore. This apparent bipolar disorder, is caused by the outside world, but necessary to overcome the challenges presented at someone that wishes to break his karmic cycles and transform his life.

Normal is not normal anymore. The vast majority of the people are freaks. That is why love is overrated. You can't love someone who doesn't know what that is, when you have surpassed the overall system of the masses and are not any longer dependent on it.

Chapter 19: How to Use Trauma to Your Advantage?

It is not a coincidence that great personalities had traumatic childhoods, because you have to endure a large amount of pain at a young age to be immune to it when you grow older.

This doesn't mean that you won't get angry, depressed, frustrated, sad, and afraid, but rather that you don't allow these emotions to stop you.

The same applies to love. It is foolish to support the many claims that a business owner must be lonely and not develop strong relationships while working on his business idea. But it's equally foolish to assume that most people will agree to support you on your dreams. They won't!

The ideal balance, of encountering people and selecting them, allowing them to enter our life and eventually break our heart, is difficult to be achieved, but not impossible, once you have the right knowledge and training.

This is what my books offer you — a way of strengthening your mind and spirit.

In this sense, comparing your life to mine, will seem much easier. Applying what I write here, to most people, is actually much easier than it is to me. And, likewise, it is only normal that your results far surpass my own.

My karmic cycles change too fast for any common person to handle. So many times, people cry in front of me, just by hearing me describe my life.

For most people, their karmic cycles are longer and more stable. That makes it easier to create significant changes and obtain long term positive results.

The vast majority can't even handle me speaking about my own life. It's too much for their mind and emotions. They get nervous, start to panic, and sometimes, they even avoid me, to avoid such emotions.

They manifest much more stronger reactions to my own experiences than I do. I simply go over them as it if was just another battle in my endless war.

Furthermore, it is interesting to see that, although my relationships typically last a few months or weeks, the ones of the men and women I help, last many years, even a lifetime.

I have helped really many people in finding the love of their life. Because, you see, comparatively, most people are not ambitious enough to get the world to hate them.

You should be happy to notice everyone hating you when you are doing something of value, because it means it's also very important for the future of mankind.

The two areas in which I was insulted the most, was the music and book industry; and it was also in these two areas that I won many awards.

Nobody ever tried to insult me in martial arts, because I wasn't planning to compete; nobody insulted me as a business consultant, because I was making others rich; and so on.

You need to be making extraordinary changes in the universe of others to see insults coming.

When I started receiving many attacks from other authors, that's when I knew I had found my life purpose.

What I want to tell you with these stories, is that you don't necessarily want to be more spiritual. Being more spiritual implies attracting more profound pains, more enemies on the side of love, and more loneliness.

What you do want, is to balance your current life, or attract abundance. Then, you will have more freedom to make the right choices and without regrets.

You will never regret any decision, if you know that you made the right one.

If you want more from life, please always consider all the implications.

Chapter 20: How to Simplify Your Plans?

Our existence can be explained by a tridimensional approach to it. This way of analyzing reality, allows us to consider our problems from different perspectives, all of which complement one another.

If we place God on the top, our own will has to be represented by one of the corners, while our ideal self will be the other. This is how we design the three angles of approach to life.

In the Catholic church, these three views, are named Father, son and holy spirit. But the concepts are too abstract for the common minds to reach them. Even though, we have here the son representing the ideal self, and the holy spirit as the energy moving the self.

Whatsoever is the geometric form used to study reality, we will come to the conclusion that we can't become our ideal version unless it is possible to coordinate this ideal with a higher power — a higher reason or motive. And how can you connect with this higher power unless you express your ideal self to Him?

You see, these three approaches are interdependent. If you want to control your own mind, you have to use it towards an ideal future, an ideal reality, a dream or project of your own.

You can do this by closing your eyes and imagining yourself talking to a group of friends, and telling them about your achievements, being such achievements related to everything you want.

Your brain patterns will change just by doing this exercise regularly, making it easier for you to think according to your desired outcome.

You can actually increase the level of difficulty in this exercise, by doing the same with people you already know.

Simply imagine a conversation with them while having your eyes closed, and telling them about what you have, as in being everything you wish to have.

One of the things you will immediately notice, with this exercise, is that it's easier to imagine yourself talking about your dreams to some people than others. And that's how your mind unveils who you must let go from your life, and who you should spend more time with.

Another thing that you will notice, is that it's easier to mention some dreams rather than others. This, because your potential to achieve those dreams is higher than your potential to acquire the others. And that's how your mind unveils which skills you lack the most, and which ones you need to develop, if you truly want to be able to reach for anything in life.

In regards to this last situation, if you feel overwhelmed by the experience, you can overcome it by simply repeating the exercise every day, and until your brain eventually fabricates the necessary thinking patterns that allow you to believe that you have the potential to acquire that which seems unattainable at the moment, i.e., the circumstances and necessary amount of wealth that will lead you to the skills you need to develop.

The advantage of repeating this exercise, is that it leads you to a constant transmutation, by focusing on the other two elements of this reality-triangle.

You see, our mind develops patterns based on emotions, and those emotions emerge from our own reality and personal experiences. If we are not entirely happy with the person we have become and what we have, we can't force that happiness either. We need to develop first the mental structure that will allow the attraction of what we want.

This attraction has a magic component to it, that can be attributed to God. But as mentioned before, reality operates with the law of the triangle, therefore it needs one side of this triangle to manifest — which appears as your own actions through the other side — as being what the world gives you.

The more prepared you are to accept new challenges, the easier it will be to recognize opportunities in your environment.

The better you are at closing this gap — of opportunities and actions — the faster you come to your objectives.

Chapter 21: Why Some People Will Always Fail?

The ones who refuse my knowledge, even when it matches what they are seeking to know, are, quite simply, people who don't trust themselves enough to obtain what they want.

That is why they fail in one side of the triangle of manifestations, even though the other two elements are there, i.e., God sending them to me, and me offering them the answers.

As a famous Guru said, "what you gather is not the problem. Your ability to use what you want is the question" (Jaggi Vasudev).

Thus, the transformation of any reality begins with the transformation of the inner world that is made of our beliefs.

A famous billionaire reinforced this fact, when he said: "When the student is ready, the master appears, but if the student doesn't learn, the master leaves" (Tai Lopez). And in this last quote, you have a resume of what occurs when one manifests without the responsibility to act.

To change the circumstances, we must apply a continuous visualization of an imagined future in spite of anything in our present rejected reality, that, nonetheless, we need to learn to differentiate, so that the opportunities coming our way aren't lost. But we do need to act on that differentiation by accepting the opportunities to challenge and change ourselves.

It does not matter how much money we have, what level of education we have, or even the knowledge we possess. It does not matter how beautiful or ugly we are either, or how young or old we are. There is not one single barrier that can justify not manifesting what seems impossible. The most important barriers are within us.

You only block yourself from obtaining something when you allow someone else to tell you that it's not possible; When you choose to believe that person.

All my life, and even now, after manifesting one of my most difficult achievements, I heard people telling me that books don't sell. Everyone said it and everyone still says it. But for the past six years of my life, I am a full-time author and I have been traveling the world with the money I make from what I write.

I have published over 300 books, and again, everyone tells me that it's not possible.

Before, I was seen as crazy, and now I am seen as a liar, or, at best, a scam artist, fooling millions of naive readers from around the globe with books I "invent", as I was told. And yet, my own personal world doesn't change because of what the rest thinks. Although they do force me to assume that I am living between parallel universes - the commonly shared insanity and the truth, that apparently, only I experience and see.

I have done many impossible things in my life. Every single time, every single person told me that it couldn't be done. Once I did it, I was called lucky.

When MTV music television awarded me, I was called lucky too, after defeating millions of music producers in a world competition.

You will never get the credit deserved from the vast and extremely stupid masses. They live in a very small world of their own. And they are, as you can see from my examples, schizophrenic.

If you allow them to dictate what is possible or not, you will reduce yourself to their world, and lose plenty of what was already destined to you at birth.

People have this illusion, that when the odds are in their favor, they have more chances of achieving success, until a car crashes and they die, or someone stabs a knife on them to get a few coins, or they die from stroke.

Life is too short and fragile to consider the odds.

If you want to improve your odds, ignore the odds. That's how I get what I want.

YOUR FULL POTENTIAL

I don't care that more than 80% of the authors alive in the world today can't make more than $1000 a year. I don't care that only 1% to 10% of them can make a living from their books. I don't care about what people think I should or shouldn't be writing or how. I really don't care about any of that. And yet, I always get losers telling me that I should care more about what they think. Why? Why should I listen to a loser?

When everything fails, people will blame me for not having compassion for them.

Most people want compassion for no reason. They think they were born entitled to get respect and love. And yet, that's not how life works.

Most people are insane and all of their actions and behaviors are towards justifying their insanity. And as hard as it seems, success is a lonely road, because you just can't get both worlds at once. You are either the successful entrepreneur and the awarded artist, or you are the lucky and crazy unfriendly one they wish they never met, showing them what a pathetic existence they live.

Chapter 22: Why Do We Attract What We Don't Want?

I have continuously manifested money when I needed it. I have made my dreams come true. I have attracted the exact partners I wanted in my life. And I have also attracted my own experiences.

What I could not control was the outcome of such experiences in me as an individual.

We can't control what others do with what we offer them. Many times, once we attract what we want, a change is necessary in us for it to perpetuate in time. And that's when we need to make our most important decisions.

If the woman in my life wants to get married, but refuses to support me in my goals, and doesn't show the necessary level of commitment to the relationship, I don't really care about her explanations or excuses. I have to end the relationship that I attracted.

There is no other way, because I can't force her to change, and to expect it, will merely increase the speed of this process. She will be unhappy if I force her into a life she doesn't want, even when she wants the same outcome as me, and she will create the quarrels that will end the relationship, as well as attract the situations for it to happen.

The two things — outcome and process, aren't separated.

Many women want rich men, for example, but aren't mature enough to live without the attention of their man, aren't responsible enough to take care of their life on their own, and quite often, are too infantile to be left alone without the potential to cheat on their relationship.

As a matter of fact, plenty of the things that are praised in today's world, represent the most degrading and infantile aspect of it. But an undesirable future is also the result of what was created by the absence of self-determinism.

This insufficient self-determinism, then manifests in the form of a weak manifestation. And, in this sense, I certainly can't say I'm perfect in applying what I know. I have failed many times, and my own experiences also taught me plenty about my own limitations and needs.

Rarely is success immune to failure. Many of the greatest entrepreneurs have failed tremendously and plenty throughout their entire life, and before succeeding.

Many others, got nothing else but only failure. We just don't get to hear their stories.

Nobody wants to hear stories about failure, even though they are equally important as the stories about success. It is failure that leads to success.

Success without failure is called luck.

As we change our fate, we need to confront our own values, and know what we can or can't accept. And I know for sure what type of people and lifestyles I can't accept.

There are things that people have done to me in their past, that I can't forgive, even if I try. And there are things I can't forget from my own memories. And so, everything that I have attracted brought forwarded my own insecurities as well as my certainties about what I really need and want form life.

One of the things I had to realize, was that money wasn't one of them. I.e., I put more importance in my art — the books I write and the music I compose and produce than I put on the businesses I create or support.

Everything is important to me, but when it comes the moment to weight the level of importance I give to certain paths, only books and music fill my life with such a strong meaning, that nothing else matters.

Chapter 23: Why You Shouldn't Feel Ashamed?

I could work in seven business at the same time, when I was in a relationship with a girl that wanted to get married and leave her job. But once she cheated, nothing made sense anymore.

I stopped all that work without blinking my eyes, and without any regrets. But, I then returned to my books and music to recover emotionally.

Not everyone is the same. As you go through life, you will see that some things always take more importance for you than others and for different reasons, that you can't always verbalize or justify to others.

For those that have a 9 to 5 job they hate, it's perfectly understandable that, as they say, the "sons and daughters mean the world". Men who often don't have much going on in their life also suffer more with their breakups than those who are too busy to cry.

When you are too busy creating a new world for yourself, you don't really have time to suffer. You do, but you just don't stay there, focused on the pain and the memories.

One of my latest girlfriends told me once that she used to spend the weekends crying when we are apart, and to which I replied: "because you have nobody to take you to clubs to get drunk and find someone else to have sex with". And she immediately shut her mouth, because this was the truth.

She wasn't crying because of me; she created our fights. She even admitted it was all her fault.

She was crying because there was nothing meaningful going on in her life apart from me and what I gave her; and she was putting this burden on me and blaming me for it, even though she was the one pushing me apart, ending it all, finally, with the ultimate betrayal, when she found another man.

She destroyed a three years relationship with a business owner and author, to fall in an illusion that lasted one month only, before she tried to get me back.

You can't heal the stupid. It's probably one of the worse and saddest of all diseases. Because the stupid often don't know they are stupid.

The problem here is that we all have limited time and limited potentialities. Three years is a lot of time to invest in someone who is stupid.

You can't just give so much attention to someone who is not responsible enough not to get drunk every Friday night. You can't play such games when you are trying to move your life forward.

The large majority of the women don't get the best men, but the worse, because the best men are too busy to take care of immature adults. And most women are too busy with their appearance to know how to be a wife. They want the marriage part but not the responsibilities that it brings with. And yet, you don't just attract a new reality but also a new version of yourself to match it. Hardly can you change your life without changing yourself.

Yes, this applies to me as well. I attracted an immature person and kept her for too long, because I wasn't strong enough to stop her from chasing me every time we had disagreements.

I never met a man that is able to refuse a very attractive women either. So, the experience, did make me stronger.

One part can't be accepted without the other, because, as explained before, they are interconnected. As a matter of fact, one thing that I constantly noticed in all new entrepreneurs, was that it wasn't necessarily the idea or the product or even the strategy that made them fail, but their lack of willingness to change themselves.

You simply can't succeed, if you don't develop a personality to match what you want. It doesn't matter how strong your motivation is, or how much you apply the law of attraction and visualizations. It won't happen.

YOUR FULL POTENTIAL

I know a person that is highly motivated for nearly twenty years in his business idea and sold nothing, because he refuses to adapt to the real world around him. He thinks he is a business owner but he is a nobody. He does not possess the determinism to make things happen. He is too slow, too lazy and too stupid.

There are other people I know, that lack the opportunities, and when such opportunities appear, often through me, and I send them in the form of questions, they take weeks, if not months, to reply me, again justifying their misery.

The best entrepreneurs I know, are not afraid of changing. On the contrary. They change very fast, after asking me how.

Either they know or not this spiritual law, they are applying it.

Many times, such successful entrepreneurs don't even consider money but only opportunities.

In one of the recent cases, a Chinese friend asked me to help him with the marketing of one of his companies, in exchange for selling products from my own companies in China through his other companies.

Chapter 24: How to Challenge the Odds?

It is as important that someone says to you, "I think you're not a good person", as it is "I think you are a bad person".

What people say is their opinion, but how you respond is yours in relation and always to theirs.

It is for this reason that I disregard any praise that people may give me. It is as important to me that they say that I am a good person, as it is that they say I am bad; it is as important to me that they say that I write good books, as it is that they say I write bad books.

I am not saying with this, that I don't care about being praised. Naturally, and as anyone else, I do enjoy having this type of attention. But I do not convince myself of my worth, or lack of it, in relation to others.

I would be in a bad situation financially, if I did not know how to measure such worth on my own and effectively.

What I do and who I am, is guided by specific values. If I am being recognized or not by those values, is not relevant. It is relevant only that I follow them.

This said, if I do know that my work is good, it doesn't matter that thousands of people can't see that. It matters only that there are those who can.

We don't necessarily break a negative karmic cycle by attacking it, but by analyzing the causes and looking at our purpose beyond it. And, through this angle of observation, I do know what a good author is, I know that I want to follow the right values to keep being one, and I know why I want it. Everything else becomes irrelevant before this evidence.

My emotions, do matter, and so, I want people to like me. But if I let my emotions take value ahead of my moral principles, such as sharing value in my books, and improving them in any way I can, to increase the level of trust I receive, then what I do has no meaning.

This is what happened to many celebrities, that allowed their fame to dictate their career.

They then wonder why they don't have any more inspiration.

They lost it because they lost themselves too along the way.

Our "problems cannot be solved at the same level of thinking that created them" (Albert Einstein), but the nature of the problems does transform towards the modification of our thought patterns. This is why it is so important to follow the right values.

Chapter 25: Why Do People Lie to Themselves?

When you allow yourself to follow a speaker, author, celebrity, entrepreneur, that has not guided himself or herself by the right values, you become lost and without knowing why.

When the bible mentions wolves in sheep clothing, it is not referring only to priests of false religions, but anyone that, in the name of good, does something evil.

This evil consists in breaking the language of God into pieces, and then leading you and others towards a path of self-deception.

The difference between good and evil can he identified through sacred geometry, also known as the mathematics of nature, because this is how you elevate yourself.

This sacred geometry is present in music too, as well as in divination methods. It's universal. And it's how we detect that which builds us or destroys us.

I can look at the words of any speaker and writer, and clearly identify where he is fooling people, simply because I use what I just said in all of my books and quotes to elevate those who follow me.

It is only natural that, if I use a certain method every day, I will be good at identifying those who use the same method and those who don't, or those who use such method to deceive the masses, which is even worse.

If you follow the wrong speakers and writers, you may then believe that you are fighting against others, or a spouse, or simply failing in achieving your dreams, when in fact, you have been deceived towards the wrong ideals.

For example, what does the idea of "independent woman" truly gave women? Isolation and loneliness. Because there is nothing wrong about depending on another person.

The key word to look at here is trust, and not independency. Because you don't consider independency when you have trust. It's only when you lack trust that your own will becomes more important. But if you disregard trust, guess what happens? A higher divorce rate.

Marriage is always a relation of codependency. But, once you distort the meaning of old values, and then make it a taboo to openly discuss them, it's difficult to fix any misunderstandings along the way. And this sets the stage for any liar to introduce himself as a helper and be easily accepted. That's why the masses are easily brainwashed.

One of the most popular liars of all — Eckhart Tolle, for example, has damaged the brain of, at least, two former girlfriends of mine, and enough for them to be convinced that his theories are good.

To this day, they can't see how they keep sabotaging their own results by following such author.

Somehow, people become blind to the obvious, when a certain author fits delusional belief patterns. But he is not the only one. There are many famous writers and speakers doing the exact same thing.

That's also, basically, how many governments take advantage of women's rights to charge more taxes and control the population at an earlier age.

That's also how many business owners, psychologists and psychiatrists make a profit out of women's depressions.

Above all, this mass misery, is making the pharmaceutical companies, much richer every year.

You see, there is much to gain from women's misery and illusions. But not much from their happiness. That's why feminism is used against them and certain authors get a recognition that, to a great extent, has been fabricated.

YOUR FULL POTENTIAL

Most people are too naive to believe that big companies like Amazon and Google manipulate the search engines, to give them what they should be reading, according to the standards imposed from above, rather than showing what the market truly has to offer.

If you type the whole title of my books on both platforms, you will hardly find them. But you will get at the top many others, that aren't even related to what you wrote.

Free will and choice are both illusions. Nobody has them. What people do have is the illusion of having them.

If you focus on the topic of "independency" in particular, you will notice that the deception here came in the form of a distortion of the concept. Because you do want to be independent, but that's not where you want to focus. Your focus should be on trust.

There is no point in being independent with someone you can't trust. But there is a great value in being independent with someone you trust. However, when you are independent with someone you trust, do you really care if sometimes you are being dependent, codependent or independent?

No, you don't care, because when you are with someone you really trust, those things become irrelevant. You know that, whatever happens in your life, that other person will watch over you.

Do you see now, how billions of women were deceived, by breaking moral values into parts and then reorganizing them for new purposes? That's actually how deception often works.

Most of what Eckhart Tolle, and many others, write or say, when broken into parts that can be analyzed individually, and in relation to many other parts and thinking patterns, clearly reveal the falsehood and the traps behind the structure of the sentences.

However, the masses don't know how to do this effectively. The educational system did not prepare them to do that either.

They are deceived by their own emotions.

Few are the readers who go through many famous authors, then find me, and realize the huge difference.

It takes a tremendous analytical capacity to do that, after so much reading, reason why most of them are either physicians or entrepreneurs, or even freemasons.

The rest of the population will never see the cause of their own misfortune as being in following the wrong beliefs. Simply because those falsehoods provide them with comfort. And they are scared of moving outside that comfort zone.

In medieval times, leaving the comfort zone was labeled as "heresy" and many were burned alive for doing it. In today's world, people are scared of very little when compared to those times.

We didn't change much on our perception of religion either. In spirituality, one of the most common misunderstandings comes from the idea that the purpose of life is to do and think what you want, because God loves us all. But where is the place for moral action then?

That's why so many religious people are immoral and disrespectful. Millions and millions, have been led astray by the wrong religious values.

The masses will never see the value of what I write because their level of consciousness is too low to perceive this level on understanding. They will continue to follow the wrong authors, and fail in life. Only those who have read through many of such authors, and realized the consequences of their mistakes, can recognize a good author when they find one.

In other words, with a higher level of responsibility, also comes a higher form of awareness. So don't expect the right values from mediocre minds. Once you elevate yourself, you will naturally notice which authors and leaders are at the same level, and which ones are not. Your capacity to accept that, is what will set you free.

Chapter 26: How to Be Rich and Spiritual?

When we think of problems, money is often the first coming to mind, and it follows indeed the patterns of many other types of problems.

Now, the topic of money may seem irrelevant when talking about religion, but hardly will a poor person understand God, because his life is composed of a great deal of suffering and struggling.

It is the rich person who will tell you that it doesn't matter which religion you follow, if you don't have the right values. And that's why it's easier for those whose life's stability depends on faith, to properly identify God.

There is no problem in changing your perception of your own religion, when you acquire a higher level of understanding of the moral values that bring you closer to God.

God does not have a religion; He or She, or It, or Them, did not create any, and did not show public support to any either. All of these things are fabrications of mankind. Therefore, you are not rejecting God when rejecting a religion. What you are really rejecting is mankind's perceptions of God and religion.

According to the rules that govern the dynamic energy of life, if we find differences in existential problems, it is only because we believe that we're able to analyze them from different angles. And we often do, we shift our perspective on reality, only to understand it. That's how we elevate ourselves, in our spirituality and also in our ability to achieve financial success.

Sadly, however, that is also how so many people get trapped in mental illnesses. The very popular Narcissistic Personality Disorder, for example, is nothing more than a shift of roles between aggressor and victim, that perpetuates the victimhood in a state of aggression, if that makes any sense.

It does make sense to the one who sees herself as a victim of her own movie. It's like directing a movie, playing all the actors and still complain about how it ends.

A big portion of the differences that we see in the world, in the form of religion, politics and even values, is just the result of a tribalistic mindset in which we build a reality to match our own better. And this reality provides us with new challenges, only because we've shown ourselves ready to face them when shifting our attitude with such exclusivity.

All the problems that we face are proportional to our attitude towards attracting them. And so, one can say that we never face problems bigger than our true and most complete self.

Whenever you overcome this self, new problems emerge to match it. But the same occurs when you try to escape it. So you don't really avoid problems, but merely change their nature.

Good problems are, for example, having too much knowledge to analyze, too many people pretending to be your friend, and not knowing where to keep your money safe.

Bad problems, would be, for example, assuming that your religion is better than others, and you don't know how to defend yours against theirs, or to assume that the problem you have is in your gender, race, or nationality.

Chapter 27: How to Think Effectively?

The less capable humanity is of integration, the more differences it will appear to have.

All the complexities of the world are a product of a lack of capacity to absorb the differentiations. Humans systematically create new labels for new situations that they can't understand.

This behavior pattern appears endlessly and it's for this reason that most people possess so many challenges in life that, although appearing to be distinct from one another, entertain their spirits with a sense of normality. But to suffer or face depression and loss shouldn't feel normal to anyone.

Now, surely, we can say that suffering is part of life, but just because there are wars going on doesn't mean we need to fight them. Although we live within a system that compels us to live within its norms, the real purpose of life, from a spiritual perspective, consists in the rebellion of the spirit through the systematization of its own existence in higher norms, or by acquiring more meaningful moral values.

That, however, doesn't' happen, unless one has been educated or educated himself on the boundaries of the world in which he exists, and which rarely happens, because, generally speaking, most people feel comfortable in following the norms of this same world.

The comfort is another side of this trap, as it eventually consumes time, then energy and finally our attention.

Basically, the world is designed to self-destroy itself, through the consumption of the energy of those who live in it. Even our own body becomes consumed by earth once its days come to an end.

A true spiritual life would then have to be one in which we move in the opposite direction. But what sense does that make if we start to argue about the meaning of death or the concept of heaven?

Philosophically speaking, it may make no sense, but from a spiritual perspective, if reincarnation is real, it makes all sense. And that's why most people are scared of debating and scientifically analyzing reincarnation. For if they prove it real, everything else will have to conjugate in the same direction.

The risk of being wrong is simply too high for the vast majority. And so they accept their state of mental slavery gladly.

In other words, one only solves his problems by focusing on the conscious creation of his fate.

There is no way to avoid the fact that, the one who is not actively working towards his own spiritual freedom, will become imprisoned in the system of ideas and values of the physical world, a system created by other delusional minds, with their own fears and interests too.

It's simply not possible to worship the true God and the world. The two systems of values are currently incompatible.

Humanity would have to elevate itself for that to become a possibility, which, due to the energies of the planet itself, is also now an impossibility. Maybe in a distant future, or a distant planet, that can be easier to occur.

For now, the only possibility comes in the form of an ascension of the spirit.

Chapter 28: How to Solve Any Problem?

The first step to eliminate any problem consists in the removal of our attention from it. But how can we then understand it and avoid a repetition? After all, if we attracted a certain outcome first, we are likely to attract it again in a near future.

In order to understand your problem, you need to remove first your emotional connection to it. You do this by analyzing the emotions that you feel when thinking about it.

You can simply ask yourself: "How I you feel?"; and: "why?"

Proceed to repeat this question to yourself, until all the emotions vanish.

Inevitably, the more you repeat this exercise, the more other memories, associated with this problem in particular, will come to the surface.

You may eventually realize that the real reason why you attracted a certain problem, was because you hold a belief within you, set many years into the past.

Someone may have told you that you would always be poor, or that you don't deserve to be loved, or that life is a struggle and people are evil. Whatsoever it was, it became suppressed deep enough for you not to see how you have led yourself into the same cycle of issues, while reinforcing that belief.

Quite often, when people eliminate some problems, they create new ones, similar to the previous, because this is how the mind is designed to protect itself while adjusting to the environment.

We all have an animal side and a spiritual side. To say that we are just intelligent animals is to neglect that spiritual side. And one cannot overcome the animal side without understanding and experiencing his spiritual side.

That spiritual side comes in the form of consciousness, and it is with consciousness that we awake, and literally shift our life towards a better outcome.

It is very hard for atheists to do this. Because they depend only on their intellect and the mind is attached to the physical experiences of the material world.

One cannot overcome the mind without the qualities of the spirit.

Many people live under the spell that the mind contains all the answers to life. And it is called a spell, because they are constantly presented with facts proving them otherwise.

They then neglect these facts, no matter how abundant, and call the creators of such realities, lucky.

There is a vast amount of excuses created to reject the spiritual side of life. But the fact remains that, without it, one moves in circles, never finding himself or his full potential.

Chapter 29: How Can Negativity Be Good for You?

Like children, many adults create problems so that they can discover the meaning of life and who they are, and they do this by provoking others. Those behaviors do create effects, but not quite the ones one should expect.

There is no point in proving that people are selfish and evil, unless you are filtering a large group in order to find the ones who are not, and are then willing to associate yourself with those people.

Likewise, what is the purpose of saying that love is an illusion, if you cannot find the ones that are not living under that illusion?

You see, there is nothing wrong with making our wildest beliefs a reality, if they fulfill us and lead many others to a better existence.

For example, becoming a full-time writer is often perceived as an impossibility for many, but I did it, and I am much happier with myself and my life now, and even happier when I receive messages from readers telling me that their life improved with my wisdom. In this case, we are witnessing something that is discarded by many as a very useful element in their life. And I am not referring to me in particular, but the manifestation of my dream.

We can be more practical and address the fact that once the automobile was invented, many horse owners went out of business. And yet, we can't deny that the automobile dramatically improved our life quality.

I am not saying that all problems have a positive side, as many claim, but rather that problems are only useful when they fuel us in the direction we must go. Because not all problems necessarily present the opposite version of them as being positive.

In many cases, the only positive thing to do is to reject the whole context of the problem in the first place.

As an example of this, there is our nationality. Wherever I go, I must tell people where I was born and present a passport, but I completely rejected that country. I don't have any bank account there, I don't own property there, I even stopped talking to most people I met there, and I almost never visit it anymore. I don't even like to talk about it, because it feels like I am promoting it, whenever I mention it. I want nothing to do with it. And yet, people find this strange, as if my birth conditioned my entire existence and identity as a human being.

This is absurd, but it does explain the way most people think. The vast majority have as many attachments to their identity as they have to their birth country. They cannot change, quite simply, because they assume that who they are right now, is who they will always be.

In other words, instead of addressing our problems to understand our spiritual identity, we must go directly to our spirit to understand those problems; and we do that by moving through them and rejecting any form of mental attachment to the physical world.

We cannot change the fact that most people can't love, but we can seek those who do. We can't change our nationality, but we can live in a place where that doesn't matter. We can't change the color of our skin, but we can associate ourselves with those who look at us as human beings, rather than a subspecies of the human race.

The same can be said about love. I have had many arguments with people over appearance and age. Some say I am too old to date young women, others say that I should date older women, some say I am ugly, and others that I am attractive. But my point here is that, if I spend my time analyzing what people say about me, I will waste my energies on the process and reach no results or conclusions. Or maybe I would achieve conclusions that wouldn't serve me.

Here, the solution is the same that you must apply to the anatomy of any problem. You must first define what you want, and then refuse to apologize for wanting it.

YOUR FULL POTENTIAL

Maybe you need to meet twenty thousand people, before you can find one that thinks you are beautiful, worth of respect and admiration. But isn't the search worth it?

God did not create a world in which everyone fits a specific box of concepts. Humans did that. Therefore, the more you conceptualize yourself, the less potential you will have to reach for the things you pray for.

It is ok to hate that which is supposed to be hated. You just need to choose wisely.

Chapter 30: How to Identify Your True Nature?

Our thoughts are nothing but a structure formulated by the mind and reinforced by our social system.

That allows those at the top to easily program us with their set of values and guidelines, being the educational system the most well-structured formal entity for this purpose. And naturally, this same system excludes creativity from it.

Most of the educational programs exclude the arts, and yet, the most successful ones include them as a priority. And this paradox leads us to the inevitable fact that knowledge is systematically outsourcing elements of reality. We depend on it in order to create but we don't create because of it. It is only with the potential to dream and be ambitious that this occurs.

Therefore, it is not a coincidence that the more people are imprisoned in an outdated social system, the more they will suffer with depression and the lack of fulfillment of their life goals. Depression is actually becoming more predominant in children and teenagers born into a world that doesn't fit them anymore.

The reason why things are like this, comes from the predisposition of the human race to be arrogant and predatory. In other words, the hierarchical control of things as they present themselves, always favor those at the top.

The new type of stupidity is actually coming from the abundance of useless knowledge, accumulated by the academics who are supposed to maintain the system as it is, rather than change it.

Most of what is produced in the Universities today, consists in understanding humanity well enough to control it, rather than study its natural and necessary changes. Even when someone changes beyond the boundaries of his or her own group, a conflict emerges. And this, because, to a great extent, our individuality only starts beyond the concept of tribe, and for most people their tribalistic instincts, or need for security, are still a very strong component of their psyche, determining their overall thinking.

There is a strong emotional power in the nationality, the name, the family and the global idea one has of himself based on his background. You have to discard all that to finally begin identifying the real personality in you.

It may seem like a misfortune for those who have lost it all in their life, and have even been betrayed by the ones whom they loved the most, but if you look at things from this angle, it may very well be an opportunity to restart life in a correct path.

Those who aren't destined to great things have the easiest existence. For them everything seems logical, because they were never pushed towards necessary transformations.

Few are the animals who need to outgrow their shell. Most simply grow in it. Likewise, most people act in defense of their own mental structures, assimilating what can only benefit them or, in other words, benefit their structures.

We always deny what we can't understand, so we can't expect that, in a disagreement, one of the individuals may abdicate of his mental structures. It's a scary idea.

On the other hand, the need for "physical evidence" is the biggest impediment to a spiritual recognition that implies a shift in the thinking patterns. One hardly upgrades his life, unless he is capable of growing beyond his beliefs.

About the Publisher

This book was published by the 22 Lions Bookstore.
For more books like this visit www.22Lions.com.
Join us on social media at:
Fb.com/22Lions;
Twitter.com/22lionsbookshop;
Instagram.com/22lionsbookshop;
Pinterest.com/22LionsBookshop.